W9-DDJ-465

AMERICA'S GREAT POLITICAL FAMILIES

THE ROOSEVELTS

BY ROBERT GRAYSON

CONTENT CONSULTANT
NANCY BECK YOUNG
DEPARTMENT CHAIR AND PROFESSOR
DEPARTMENT OF HISTORY, UNIVERSITY OF HOUSTON

Essential Library

An Imprint of Abdo Publishing | abdopublishing.com

abdopublishing.com

Published by Abdo Publishing, a division of ABDO, PO Box 398166, Minneapolis, Minnesota 55439. Copyright © 2016 by Abdo Consulting Group, Inc. International copyrights reserved in all countries. No part of this book may be reproduced in any form without written permission from the publisher. Essential Library™ is a trademark and logo of Abdo Publishing.

Printed in the United States of America, North Mankato, Minnesota
102015
012016

Cover Photos: AP Images, left; Pach Brothers/Library of Congress, right
Interior Photos: Strohmeyer & Wyman/Library of Congress, 5, 8; William Dinwiddie/Library of Congress, 7; Red Line Editorial, 12–13; Library of Congress, 15, 26, 45, 59; New York World-Telegram and the Sun Newspaper Photograph Collection, 21; Underwood & Underwood/Library of Congress, 29, 41, 47; Franklin D. Roosevelt Presidential Library & Museum, 32, 33, 49, 51, 71, 73, 75, 77, 94, 101; Bettmann/Corbis, 35, 66; AP Images, 57, 69, 85, 86; US National Archives and Records Administration, 64; Elias Goldensky/Library of Congress, 83; Hulton-Deutsch/Hulton-Deutsch Collection/Corbis, 97

Editor: Mirella Miller
Series Designer: Becky Daum

Library of Congress Control Number: 2015945394
Cataloging-in-Publication Data

Grayson, Robert.
 The Roosevelts / Robert Grayson.
  p. cm. -- (America's great political families)
Includes bibliographical references and index.
ISBN 978-1-62403-910-2
1. Roosevelt, Theodore, 1858-1919--Juvenile literature. 2. Roosevelt family--Juvenile literature. 3. Presidents--Family relationships--United States--Biography--Juvenile literature. 4. United States--Politics and government--Juvenile literature. I. Title.
973.91/1092--dc23
[B]   2015945394

CONTENTS

CHAPTER 1

ROUGH
RIDERS

He was president of the United States and vice president before that. He served as governor of New York and police commissioner of New York City. However, the title Theodore Roosevelt cherished the most was colonel, the military rank he held during the Spanish-American War in 1898. There, he planted the seeds that would grow into a political dynasty. His exceptional bravery under enemy fire, strength of character, and determination would become the Roosevelt legacy.

Theodore served as assistant secretary of the US Navy in 1898. At that time, tensions between Spain and the United States over Cuban independence were about to explode into all-out war. Cuba had been a Spanish colony since 1492. Freedom fighters in Cuba had tried to win

In the Spanish-American War, Theodore became a larger-than-life figure.

Cuban independence in the past, but in 1895 a group of revolutionaries started a rebellion that would eventually drag the United States into war with Spain. The United States did a great deal of trade with Cuba. The ongoing fighting between Cuban revolutionaries and the Spanish military threatened those economic interests.

With war on the horizon, Theodore strategically positioned US Navy ships so they could destroy the Spanish fleet in Cuba and other parts of the world if a conflict erupted. When peacemaking efforts failed, the United States declared war on Spain on April 25, 1898.

A Man of Action

Theodore had no intention of sitting on the sidelines. He resigned his government post and immediately gathered a group of robust volunteers to join the fight. At age 39, Theodore, who had always dreamed of the glories of battle, got a chance to test himself in combat. The regiment he built was made up of some of his closest friends. They were fiery, tough, and eager to follow Theodore anywhere.

Theodore's unit was called the First Volunteer Cavalry and nicknamed the Rough Riders because of its members' boundless energy. It was one of several regiments formed when President William McKinley issued a call for volunteers to bolster the ranks of the US Army to fight the Spanish. Only 28,000 men were serving in the army

Many of Theodore's volunteers had been cowboys and frontiersmen; some had been police officers, others athletes.

when war with Spain was declared on April 25.[1] Theodore was named lieutenant colonel of the First Volunteer Cavalry. Though he was second in command to Colonel

Leonard Wood, Theodore had a great deal of influence over the 1,000 men in the unit.

By June, the Rough Riders, along with 6,000 other US soldiers, were on their way to Cuba.[2] The plan was to capture the port city of Santiago de Cuba, the Spanish stronghold. The US Navy would bombard Spanish ships in the city's harbor. It would be supported by US ground troops and Cuban freedom fighters in a joint land operation. Their mission was to oust Spanish soldiers from the city.

US fighters, including the Rough Riders, landed on the beaches of Daiquiri, Cuba, on June 22, 1898. Daiquiri was 18 miles (30 km) east of Santiago de Cuba. The first challenge was getting ashore. Waters were rough, and piers were splintered and washing away, but eventually they made it to land. The next day, the Rough Riders and their fellow troops captured a mountain pass in the battle of Las Guasimas.

Shortly after the battle, Colonel Wood was promoted to the rank of brigadier general, and Theodore was named colonel. In the early morning hours of July 1, US troops in the mountain pass around Las Guasimas came under heavy fire. Theodore was hit in the wrist with shrapnel.

> **"I am quite content to go now and to leave my children at least an honorable name."[3]**
> —*Theodore Roosevelt, speaking about his fighting in Cuba, in a letter to a friend in August 1898*

The Rough Riders traveled to Cuba to help the United States in the Spanish-American war.

MEDAL OF HONOR

After the battle of San Juan Hill, the US Army in Cuba recommended Theodore for the Congressional Medal of Honor. The recommendation was turned down. Many historians believe the rejection was politically motivated. The outspoken Theodore had sent a letter to US Secretary of War Russell A. Alger in August 1898 after the fighting ended. He questioned why US troops were not being sent home. Alger was furious about the letter. The colonel's actions got Alger to bring the troops home. However, Alger made sure Theodore did not get the Medal of Honor. The snub was corrected on January 16, 2001, when President Bill Clinton held a special ceremony at the White House to award the highest military honor to Theodore posthumously.

He jumped on his horse and herded his soldiers into a safe area.

Theodore began giving orders, even rallying regiments whose leaders had fallen in the assault. A Spanish soldier ran onto the battlefield and tried to kill him. Theodore pulled out a revolver and shot him. That roused his troops, who were now furiously engaged in battle.

The Charge up San Juan Hill

Stunned by the US onslaught, the Spanish troops began to retreat. As Theodore reached the top of the hill, he urged his men to keep fighting. Then the colonel saw US soldiers struggling under heavy fire at nearby San Juan Hill. The Rough Riders, led by Theodore, charged up San Juan Hill, taking no prisoners.

FINAL SURRENDER

The Spanish-American War went on for a few more weeks following the battle of San Juan Hill. The US flag was raised over Santiago on July 17, 1898. A peace treaty with Spain was signed in Washington, DC, on December 10, 1898, and hostilities came to an end.

The war was a serious blow to the Spanish Empire. Spain lost much of its remaining territory around the world, including Cuba, Puerto Rico, Guam, and the Philippines.

The conflict had lasted ten weeks. As a result of the Spanish-American War, the United States established itself on the world stage as a powerful military force. US soldiers from both the North and the South served together for the first time since the American Civil War (1861–1865). African-American troops made major contributions during the war effort as well.

Beaten back and weary, the Spaniards retreated to Santiago, where they hoped to find refuge on their ships. Theodore, however, knew those ships were not going anywhere. The ships he had sent to Cuba while he was assistant secretary of the US Navy surrounded the city. Within days, the Spanish fleet was destroyed.

Newspaper accounts of the battle of San Juan Hill were breathtaking. The Rough Riders became legendary. Their leader, Colonel Theodore Roosevelt, was a national hero and suddenly the most sought-after candidate for public office in the United States.

ROOSEVELT FAMILY TREE

OYSTER BAY BRANCH

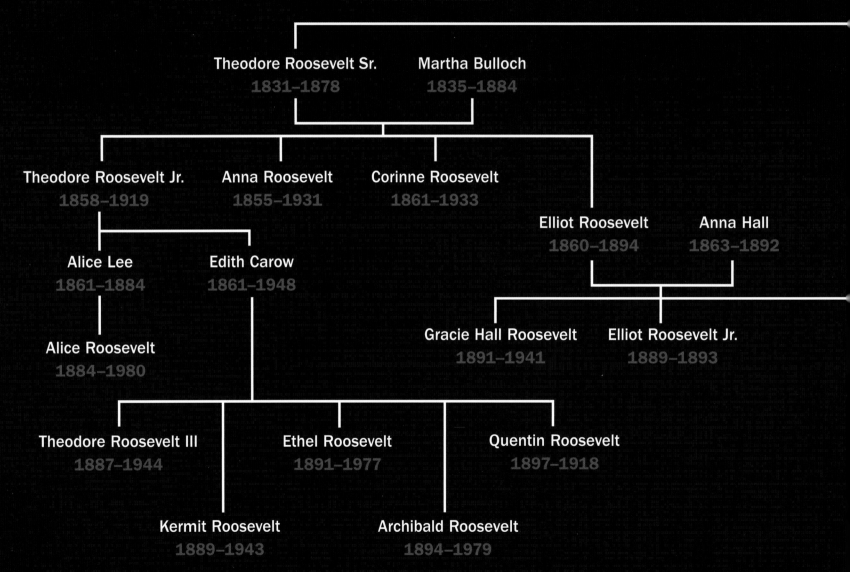

Theodore Roosevelt Sr.
1831–1878

Martha Bulloch
1835–1884

Theodore Roosevelt Jr.
1858–1919

Anna Roosevelt
1855–1931

Corinne Roosevelt
1861–1933

Elliot Roosevelt
1860–1894

Anna Hall
1863–1892

Alice Lee
1861–1884

Edith Carow
1861–1948

Alice Roosevelt
1884–1980

Gracie Hall Roosevelt
1891–1941

Elliot Roosevelt Jr.
1889–1893

Theodore Roosevelt III
1887–1944

Ethel Roosevelt
1891–1977

Quentin Roosevelt
1897–1918

Kermit Roosevelt
1889–1943

Archibald Roosevelt
1894–1979

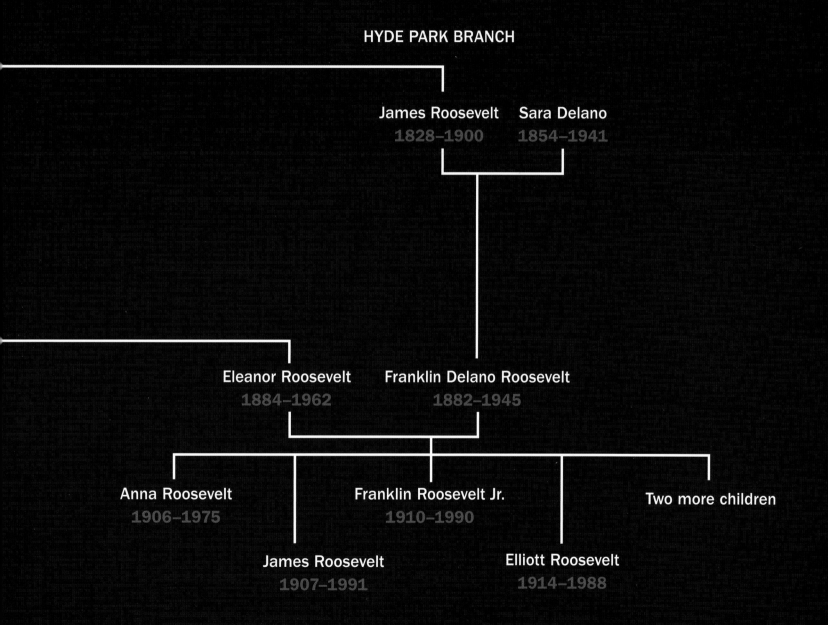

HYDE PARK BRANCH

James Roosevelt
1828–1900

Sara Delano
1854–1941

Eleanor Roosevelt
1884–1962

Franklin Delano Roosevelt
1882–1945

Anna Roosevelt
1906–1975

Franklin Roosevelt Jr.
1910–1990

Two more children

James Roosevelt
1907–1991

Elliott Roosevelt
1914–1988

CHAPTER 2

THEODORE'S WORLD

As with many well-known families in the United States, the Roosevelts can trace their roots back to a wide-eyed adventurer who came to America for all the promise the new land held. Claes Martenszen van Roosevelt, a Dutch peasant, sailed from Europe and arrived in New Amsterdam, later renamed New York, in approximately 1644. Through the generations, the family built a fortune in real estate, banking, imported glass, and West Indian sugar. They became one of the most prominent families in New York.

Early on, the Roosevelt family got involved in politics. Claes's son Nicholas was the first to use the surname Roosevelt, a shortened

The Hyde Park side of the Roosevelts lived approximately 90 miles (145 km) north of New York City.

version of the family name. He served as an alderman—much like a city councilman today—in New York City from 1698 to 1701.

Nicholas had ten children. Two of his sons, Johannes "John" and Jacobus, started the two branches of the family that would give the nation two of its most beloved presidents and an utterly adored First Lady. John was the great-great-great grandfather of Theodore Roosevelt and the great-great-great-great grandfather of Theodore's niece, Eleanor Roosevelt. Jacobus was the great-great-great grandfather of Franklin Delano Roosevelt, who married Eleanor.

The two branches of the family were identified by where they lived in the state. The John Roosevelt clan stayed in Oyster Bay on the north shore of Long Island, New York. The Jacobus branch of the family lived in Hyde Park, New York. There was another difference as well—the John Roosevelts were Republicans, while the Jacobus Roosevelts favored the Democrats.

Theodore Roosevelt Jr.

Theodore Roosevelt Jr. was born on October 27, 1858, at his parents' Manhattan town house. His father, Theodore Sr., made his fortune in the glass business. Theodore was the second of four children. He had an older sister, Anna, a younger brother, Elliott, and younger sister, Corinne.

TENSE TIMES

While some Roosevelts were Republicans and some were Democrats, the extended family was divided in other ways as well. Theodore saw some of that divisiveness in his own household. Theodore Sr. and his three brothers supported the North in the American Civil War. Theodore Sr. wanted to volunteer for military service, but his wife, Martha, begged him not to sign up.

Martha, who hailed from Georgia, favored the South. Her two brothers were in the Confederate navy. Martha feared family members might shoot at each other during the war. Theodore Sr. honored his wife's wishes and did not enter combat, but he was still a strong advocate of the Northern cause. The strain on the family eased when the war ended.

Theodore Sr. made a lasting impression on his children. He taught them to help the less fortunate by using his wealth to support a number of causes and volunteering his time each week. Theodore Sr. was one of the founders of the New York Orthopedic Hospital and the Children's Aid Society, designed to help orphans. He was also active in New York politics as a member of the Republican Reform Club. Reformers pushed for good municipal government and sought to root out public corruption.

Overcoming Challenges

Theodore was a sickly child. He suffered from acute asthma. Night after night he could hardly breathe enough to stay alive. Based on research he did, Theodore Sr. felt

POLITICS 101

Theodore was captivated by his father's role in politics. In June 1876, Theodore Sr. traveled from New York City to Cincinnati, Ohio, for the Republican National Convention (RNC). His goal was to help reformers wrestle the party's presidential nomination away from the frontrunner, Senator James Blaine of Maine. Blaine's reputation had been tarnished by a political scandal involving the Union Pacific Railroad. Theodore Sr. favored putting reformers on the national ticket.

After seven grueling rounds of voting at the convention, the reform candidate—Rutherford B. Hayes, supported by Theodore Sr. and other reformers—won the nomination for president. In the general election, Hayes beat the Democratic nominee, Samuel J. Tilden, and captured the White House. Theodore followed the political events through his father's letters and through newspaper accounts.

his son could gain control over his asthma by strengthening his body. Theodore accepted the challenge and grew stronger. The future US president never completely defeated asthma, but he learned he had the resolve to fight back.

Shortly before he turned 18 years old, Theodore entered Harvard. In addition to his studies, he wrote for the college newspaper and took up boxing, crew, football, and debate. In February 1878, during his sophomore year, Theodore was contacted to return home. His father, only 46 years old, had collapsed and died suddenly.

Haunted by Loss

After his father's death, Theodore returned to Harvard but was haunted by a deep sense of loss. When the semester ended, Theodore found comfort in the wilderness. He went hiking and hunting in the woods of Maine and regrouped. He returned to Harvard for his junior year in the fall of 1878. It was then he met 17-year-old Alice Hathaway Lee. She was the daughter of a wealthy banker from Boston, Massachusetts. At first Alice had no interest in Theodore. But soon she realized how much he loved her. They were married on Theodore's birthday on October 27, 1880, in Brookline, Massachusetts, and lived in New York City.

> **"As I saw the last of the train bearing you away, I realized what a luxury it was to have a boy in whom I could place perfect trust and confidence. Take care of your morals first, your health next, and, finally, your studies."[1]**
> —*Theodore Roosevelt Sr., in a letter to Theodore shortly after the younger Roosevelt left for Harvard University*

The marriage of Theodore and Alice was not the only wedding news to come out of the Roosevelt family in the fall of 1880. James Roosevelt I of the Hyde Park side was a lonely widow. Theodore's older sister, Anna, introduced James to a distant cousin, Sara Ann Delano, at a party in the spring of 1880. James and Sara were married that fall. They became the parents of Franklin Delano Roosevelt on January 30, 1882.

CHAPTER 3

A NEW FAMILY
BUSINESS

Theodore had studied to become a naturalist or scientist at Harvard, but now as a newlywed, he felt he needed a job that provided a more substantial income. When he returned to New York City with Alice in the fall of 1880, he enrolled in Columbia Law School. He did not stay there long, however, as law did not hold his interest. But Theodore did find something that captivated him: politics.

Theodore joined the Republican Party, as his father had, because the party had stood for a united nation under Abraham Lincoln. He viewed Lincoln as a man who was an honest reformer, and who fought for equality for all. "A young man of my bringing-up and convictions could only join the Republican Party," Theodore said.[1] He led a reform branch

Theodore became the youngest member of the New York State Assembly in 1881.

of the party in New York City. The city was heavily Democratic, and Republicans were substantially outnumbered. But Theodore was smart, young, and energetic. The Republicans wanted him to run for the state assembly seat in New York City's Twenty-First District in November 1881. He won the seat at 23 years old.

RUDE AWAKENING

When Theodore first took office in the New York State Assembly in 1882, he was astounded by the amount of corruption he found in Albany, New York's capital. "There were a great many thoroughly corrupt men in the Legislature, perhaps a third of the whole number," he later wrote in his autobiography.[2] Disturbed by that widespread corruption, he spoke about it to an uncle of his who was an influential Democrat. His uncle advised the young legislator not to fight the system but rather to go along with things as they were. Theodore refused, saying, "honesty . . . and decency . . . and administrative efficiency are the prime requisites for a legislator."[3]

Battling Corruption

The newly elected Republican legislator was determined to battle corruption and bring morality back into politics. The task would be hard. Nevertheless, Theodore fought to make elections more honest. He wanted to stop the influence wealthy businesspeople had over politicians. He was especially outraged by the patronage system, by which unqualified people got jobs in government. They were appointed to these jobs simply because they had done an elected official a favor.

Theodore did not make many friends in politics, but he did get headlines.

In January 1883, however, he found an unlikely ally. A new Democratic governor, Grover Cleveland, took office in New York. Cleveland, who was a reformer, was inspired by Theodore's ideas. He gave Theodore his blessing to reform the way civil service jobs were given out in New York. Theodore had already introduced legislation to make those changes, but it had been blocked in the assembly.

With Cleveland and Theodore working together, other reformers from both parties came out in support of changing the state civil service system. Theodore worked diligently to get the legislation passed. By the time the New York State Legislature recessed for the summer of 1883, Theodore's reforms had become law.

Theodore continued to fight corruption as the 1884 New York State Legislative session got underway in January. His wife was about to give birth to the couple's first child. During the pregnancy, Alice and Theodore lived with his mother, Martha, in New York City.

While in Albany, New York, on February 13, 1884, Theodore received two telegrams with mixed messages. One reported his daughter had been born. The second gave him the news that both his mother and wife were seriously ill. Theodore rushed home to New York City. By the time he got there, Alice was near death from kidney disease that had gone undetected. She died in the early morning hours of February 14. His mother died 13 hours later of typhoid fever.

HOME

Just after he married his first wife, Alice, Theodore purchased 155 acres (60 ha) of land in Cove Neck, New York. The couple planned to raise a large family there. In 1884, before Alice died, Theodore hired a New York City architectural firm to design a 22-room home on the property. The project continued even after Alice died and was completed in 1886. Theodore eventually moved into the home with his second wife, Edith. Theodore named the homestead Sagamore Hill, and he lived there until his death.

When Theodore was president, the press referred to Sagamore Hill as the summer White House. Guests included nieces, nephews, and even cousins from the Hyde Park side of the family. Theodore was always the center of attention at home. A master storyteller, he would entertain his guests with tales of his many adventures.

Grief Stricken Again

Theodore was devastated. He paid tribute to his wife by naming their daughter Alice. But Theodore could not be consoled. After a double funeral a few days later, Theodore felt he needed to throw himself into his work and returned to Albany. Theodore's sister Anna offered to help raise his new baby, and Theodore gratefully agreed.

Theodore decided not to seek reelection to the New York State Assembly in November 1884. With Anna taking care of Alice, Theodore went to the Badlands of North Dakota and took up ranching. Living in the rugged outdoors was exhilarating for Theodore. Yet Theodore was a New Yorker at heart and went back to the city for regular visits.

ANNA ROOSEVELT

One of the strongest members of the Roosevelt clan was Theodore's sister Anna. She had boundless energy and regularly helped her ailing mother take care of the rest of the family. Theodore often turned to Anna for counsel. Eleanor said her uncle made few decisions without getting Anna's input. Anna lived in Washington, DC, just a few blocks from the White House when Theodore was president. Theodore would often walk to her house and jokingly called her residence the "other White House."[4]

Anna did not marry until she was 40 years old. Some family members said it was because she was too busy taking care of everybody else. Anna had one son. She had a major impact on the social and intellectual development of both Alice, Theodore's eldest daughter, and Eleanor, both of whom suffered the loss of their mothers early in life.

On one of those return visits, he had a chance encounter with Edith Carow. She had been a childhood friend of Theodore's, a girl everyone thought he would marry. But as young adults they had drifted apart. Theodore started writing to Edith regularly. After two years, Theodore came to terms with his misfortune and was ready to return to New York City full time. He had also decided to court Edith.

The Republican Party came calling when Theodore returned to New York City in 1886. The party's reformers wanted him to run for mayor. Though Theodore knew it would be almost impossible to win in that Democratic stronghold, he decided to try.

Theodore lost, but the mayoral race gave him a chance to dust off his campaigning skills, speak publicly about the need to root out political corruption, and reenter New York politics after his adventures in the Badlands.

Theodore and Edith married in December 1886. After their honeymoon, the couple returned to New York City, where Theodore pursued a full-time writing career. He authored books and articles, and his literary work sold well. Writing gave Theodore the time to be with his young daughter. He soon added a son to the family as well, with the birth of Theodore III in September 1887.

Back in Politics

Theodore could not stay out of the political fray. He campaigned in the 1888 presidential election for Republican Benjamin Harrison. When Harrison won the White House,

A key role in Anna's life was serving as her brother's confidante.

THE CONSERVATIONIST

When Theodore was out west, he learned the importance of creating laws to protect open land, natural resources, and wildlife. In December 1887, he founded the Boone and Crockett Club with nine other men and served as its first president from 1888 to 1894. The club was named after well-known folk heroes Daniel Boone and Davy Crockett. The organization still exists today.

Among the club's early successes was saving Yellowstone National Park from developers and railroads. Some resorts had already been built in the park by 1888 without any regard for the construction's impact on the environment or native wildlife. Developers also planned to run a railroad right through the center of the park.

Theodore was offered a job with the new administration, civil service commissioner, in 1889. Theodore started battling corruption in the federal government, taking on anyone who got in his way. He was determined to make the way civil service jobs were awarded fair and based on merit. "Each party profited by the offices when in power and when in opposition each party insincerely denounced its opponents for doing exactly what it itself had done and intended to do again," Theodore said.[5] The reformer was back, and now he was on the national stage.

CHAPTER 4

A HERO COMES ALONG

During four years with the US Civil Service Commission, Theodore exposed and cracked down on fraud, mismanagement, and incompetence. He battled political bosses and corruption all over the nation. His investigations into civil service irregularities became legendary. "As long as I was responsible, the law should be enforced up to the handle everywhere, fearlessly and honestly," Theodore said.[1]

When President Harrison ran for a second term in 1892, he lost to Cleveland, the former governor of New York. Political bosses in both parties rejoiced, figuring they would be rid of Theodore, whom they called a "thorn in their side."[2] But Cleveland asked Theodore to stay on. The

Cleveland, Theodore, and politician David R. Francis worked closely in the early 1900s.

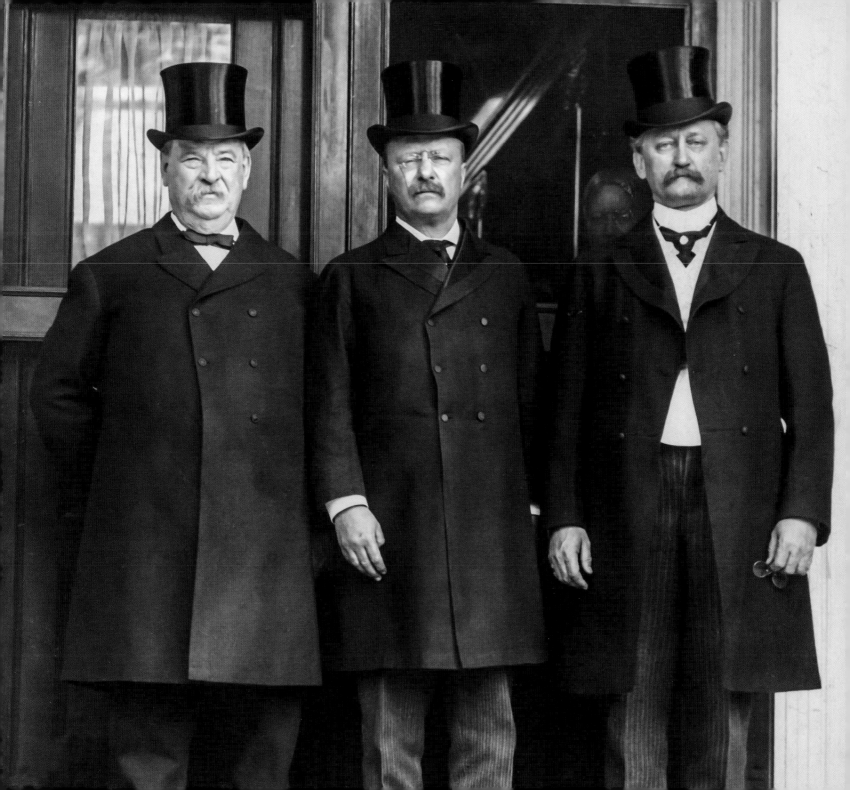

POLITICAL BOSSES

For most of his career, Theodore battled political bosses. They had complete control over a political region, dictating who got political appointments, who landed government jobs, and who ran for political office. They collected favors from elected officials, controlled financing for campaigns, and even told party members how to vote. Some political bosses held elected office; others did not. Political bosses were commonplace in US politics from the 1800s through the 1950s. Most people saw these bosses as corrupt and thought they undermined the democratic process. Many bosses engaged in criminal enterprises in addition to their political activities. Both the Democratic and Republican parties had bosses. Theodore took on the bosses of both parties.

two would work together to reform the government, just as they had in New York.

Theodore and Edith loved living in Washington, DC. They had an active social life and mingled easily with the nation's most powerful and influential people. Yet neither forgot their family ties. Not only was Theodore in continuous contact with his siblings, but he also was very much involved in their lives.

One constant worry for Theodore was his younger brother, Elliott. Elliott was a troubled soul who became an alcoholic in his early 20s. By 1891, at age 31, he was married to the socialite Anna Rebecca Hall, and they had three children. His eldest child was Anna Eleanor, known as Eleanor. He also had two sons, Elliott Jr. and Gracie Hall.

A Traumatic Childhood

Eleanor adored her father, but he was rarely home. When he was home he doted on her, and the two were very close. During his bouts with alcohol, he was away from home for long periods. Eleanor missed her father terribly during his absences. She did not get the same attention from her mother as she did from her father.

In December 1892, when Eleanor was only eight years old, her mother died of diphtheria, a serious bacterial infection, at age 29. Eleanor's brother Elliott Jr. died five months later of the same disease. Elliott had a difficult time dealing with the two deaths. Eleanor and her surviving brother, Gracie Hall, went to live permanently with their maternal

GOOD PUBLIC RELATIONS

Theodore mastered the art of good public relations. As a reformer who fought corrupt politicians, he knew it would be hard for him to gain a leadership role in party politics. The very people he was fighting ran the political parties. He brought his case directly to the public by inviting the news media to write stories about the work he was doing to reform the system. He explained why the reforms were needed and gave specific examples. Many newspaper reporters were trying to battle and expose corruption, so Theodore had plenty of support in the newsroom. The publicity made him popular, and popularity won elections. The publicity also made it hard for Theodore's opponents to keep him in line. The more they attacked him publicly, the more publicity he got. Most newspapers favored Theodore's reforms and sided with him.

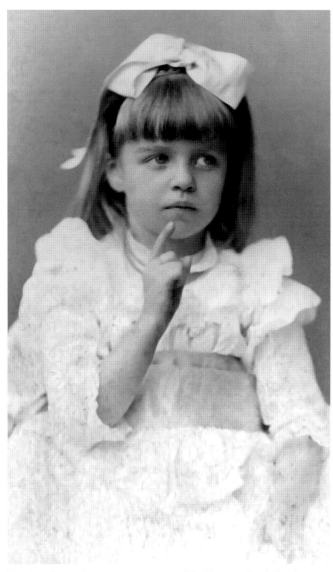

By the time she was ten years old, Eleanor had lived through the deaths of both her parents and one brother.

grandmother, Mary Ludlow Hall, in Dutchess County, New York. On August 14, 1894, Elliott died of a seizure.

Theodore was concerned about how the young girl would handle the deaths in her family. But Eleanor received a lot of support from Theodore's older sister, Anna. And Theodore looked in on her as much as he could.

Eleanor spent her time with her grandmother wisely. She read extensively, and Grandmother Hall tutored her in French and German. Eleanor studied the piano, a pursuit that fostered her passion for music. She loved the ballet and was fascinated by the idea of appearing onstage. At one point, she thought about becoming a singer. She found great pleasure in singing because her father had sung at family gatherings, and that was when he seemed to be the happiest.

Anna felt her young niece would benefit from attending Allenswood, an all-girls boarding school in London, England. She championed the idea throughout the time Eleanor lived with her grandmother. Anna herself had studied at Allenswood as a young girl and found the experience inspiring. When Eleanor's parents were alive, Anna had mentioned the idea to them, and they had visited the school while on tour in Europe. At first, Grandmother Hall did not want to send Eleanor away, preferring to oversee her upbringing and education closer to home.

A Powerful Police Commissioner

William Strong, a Republican, took office as mayor of New York City in January 1895. He asked Theodore to serve on the New York

Staying in New York gave Eleanor the opportunity to spend more time with her uncle Theodore when he came to Oyster Bay.

City Police Commission. The other three members of the commission voted Theodore president of the commission. Theodore took on corrupt police officials, making them resign. Theodore donned disguises and went out on the streets of the city to catch dishonest police officers taking bribes, leaving their posts, and meeting with known felons. He was wildly popular with the people of New York City as he relentlessly reined in the notoriously corrupt police department.

By this time Theodore was the father of five children and enjoyed being close to home in New York City. Kermit, Ethel, and Archibald joined Alice and Ted in the Roosevelt clan. Yet it was not long before leaders in Washington, DC, came calling again.

Bolstering the Navy

When Republican William McKinley became president, he wanted to put Theodore's energy to work in the nation's capital, building the US Navy into a worldwide power. He appointed Theodore assistant secretary of the US Navy in April 1897. Theodore was considered a naval expert because of the book he had written on the naval war of 1812.

Though John Davis Long was the navy secretary, he went on lengthy vacations and was more than happy to let Theodore take charge.

Theodore built up US naval strength, which was eventually put on display in the Spanish-American War. Theodore got a chance to see the fruits of his labor firsthand when he valiantly served in the war with the Rough Riders. While Theodore fought on land with his regiment, the US Navy crushed the Spanish naval fleet. When Theodore returned to the United States with the celebrated Rough Riders, he was the most famous man in the United States. Now the father of six, including his youngest son, Quentin, the whirlwind continued for Theodore.

Championing the People as Governor

On September 17, 1898, Theodore entered the race for governor of New York, and by November 8, he had easily won the post. All of the Roosevelts were thrilled with the victory. Despite their Democratic ties, the Hyde Park branch of the family voted for Theodore.

The new governor intended to move forward with his fight against corruption and his reforms to make government work for all the people of New York, especially the downtrodden. "Our attitude should be one of correcting the evils," he said.[3]

As governor, Theodore raised taxes for corporations. He raised the minimum pay for teachers, fought for an eight-hour workday for state employees, limited work hours for women and children, stepped up inspections of workplaces, and cracked down on awful working conditions. Theodore pushed for open space and clean water, addressed social welfare and consumer rights issues, and set aside forest preserves in New York State's Catskills and Adirondack regions. Theodore's work as governor of New York was keeping his name in the national spotlight. Though he thought about running for president, for the time being Theodore was content to seek another term in New York.

> **"It is hard to fail, but it is worse never to have tried to succeed."[4]**
> —*Governor Theodore Roosevelt, in a speech before the Hamilton Club in Chicago, April 10, 1899*

Eleanor Overseas

By the fall of 1899, Eleanor was on her way to Allenswood. Her aunt Anna had finally convinced Grandmother Hall that it had been Eleanor's mother's wish for her daughter to attend the prestigious school. It would turn out to be Eleanor's salvation.

At the London school, headmistress Marie Souvestre took a special interest in the shy and self-conscious 15-year-old. The headmistress inspired and challenged Eleanor. Souvestre changed Eleanor's wardrobe to reflect a more stylish look and give her confidence. She helped broaden young Eleanor's horizons, teaching her about other cultures, awakening her conscience to social injustice, sparking an interest in community activism, and getting her to follow world affairs. Her uncle Theodore

RALLYING SUPPORT

Theodore proved to be a formidable force on the national campaign trail in 1900. While running for vice president, he traveled to 24 states, mostly by train, covering more than 21,000 miles (33,800 km).[5] He went to 567 towns and made 673 speeches.[6] The sheer intensity of his campaign and his relentless attacks on his opponents impressed those who came out to see him. His speeches were described as fiery and unforgettable. At the start of the campaign he told party members, "I am as strong as a bull moose and you can use me to the limit."[7]

would soon be a key figure in those world affairs.

Shortly after Eleanor arrived at Allenswood, the United States suffered the loss of its vice president, Garret Hobart, who died of a heart attack on November 21, 1899. President McKinley would need a new running mate in 1900.

A Reluctant Vice President

Theodore was the natural choice to be McKinley's running mate. But Theodore had no interest in becoming vice president. He felt the office did not suit his personality and talents. Despite Theodore's reluctance, the party wanted him on the national ticket. Theodore was nominated for vice president at the RNC in June 1900.

Theodore vigorously campaigned against his Democratic opponents, William Jennings Bryan and Adlai Stevenson. Large crowds turned out wherever Theodore appeared during the campaign. His popularity nationwide was undeniable. McKinley and Theodore won easily on November 6. Theodore presumably would be the Republican nominee for president in 1904. Until then, Theodore had little to do as vice president.

Then, on September 6, 1901, Theodore received word that President McKinley, who was in Buffalo, New York, had been shot. At first it looked as though McKinley would recover. However, the president took a turn for the worse, and on September 13, McKinley died.

Theodore was sworn in as the twenty-sixth president of the United States. At age 42, Theodore was the youngest president ever. "It is a dreadful thing to come into the Presidency this way," Theodore wrote his close political ally Henry Cabot Lodge.[8] A true reformer was now in the White House. Theodore insisted on courage and honesty in his administration from the outset.

THE WHITE HOUSE

One of Theodore's first actions as commander in chief was to issue an executive order changing the name of the president's residence from the Executive Mansion to the White House. He even had *White House* put on the president's stationery as part of the official address of the residence. The White House had a dreary interior when the Roosevelts moved in, and the new president and Edith began renovating it. The overhaul included building the West Wing. All of the executive offices would be housed in the West Wing instead of on the second floor of the White House. This gave the Roosevelts more living space.

CHAPTER 5

THE PEOPLE'S PRESIDENT

Industrialization was transforming the United States into a wealthy and powerful nation, but Theodore worried most people were not benefiting from the shift to industrial production. Farmers and small businesses were being edged out. A rift was developing between the rich and the working class. No regulations governed the powerful men who controlled industry in the United States. Theodore now had the power to change that, and he did.

Trust Buster

Just five months after taking office, Theodore made a move that set the tone for his presidency. He took on corporate monopolies, known

After Theodore's inauguration, he got to work making big changes in the first months of his presidency.

as trusts, established by some of the nation's wealthiest people. A prime example was Northern Securities Company, founded by financier John Pierpont Morgan and a group of wealthy associates in 1901. The goal of the trust was to gain control of all the railroads between the Great Lakes and the Pacific Ocean. In February 1902, Theodore ordered the US Justice Department to take action to break up the monopoly. The dispute went all the way to the US Supreme Court, which sided with Theodore in finding that Northern Securities Company was involved in illegal restraint of trade. Theodore considered this one of his greatest accomplishments. He became known as a "trust buster," bringing suits against more than 40 trusts, from oil and tobacco monopolies to life insurance and food monopolies.[1]

As president, Theodore proved to be a man of the people, as he had in the other government offices he had held. He showed that commitment again when he intervened in a coal miners' strike in Pennsylvania in 1902. At the time, the United States ran on coal. It heated

THE BULLY PULPIT

Bully was one of Theodore's favorite words. It was widely used in his era as an adjective to mean "superb." Theodore referred to the presidency as the *bully pulpit*. He meant the presidency was an excellent platform to advocate for an issue or an entire agenda. A speech by the president automatically attracts the attention of both the people and the media, he reasoned. The term *bully pulpit* is still used to describe the power a sitting president has to rally supporters.

homes and schools and ran trains and factories. The strike, which started in the spring, had dragged on for months. With winter approaching, Theodore put a panel in place to settle the dispute. His plan worked. The miners returned to their jobs, and enough coal was available for the winter. The panel recommended that mine operators give the miners a 10 percent pay raise with shorter work hours and better working conditions.[2] Both the miners and the mine owners accepted the recommendations.

> "I am president of all the people of the United States without regard to creed, color, birthplace, occupation, or social condition. My aim is to do equal and exact justice among them all."[4]
>
> —Theodore Roosevelt, speaking before the Executive Council of the American Federation of Labor, September 20, 1902

After the coal strike ended, Theodore said, "My action on labor should always be considered in connection with my action as regards capital, and both are reducible to my favorite formula—a square deal for every man."[3] Offering every American what he called a Square Deal became the foundation of Theodore's own presidential campaign in 1904.

Domestic and Foreign Achievements

After finishing McKinley's term, Theodore was running for the presidency in his own right. He had a highly successful track record in domestic policy. He had also put together an impressive record on foreign policy. In 1903, Theodore's treaty with

> **"I ask that your marvelous natural resources be handed on unimpaired to your posterity. We are not building this country of ours for a day. It is to last through the ages."**[6]
> —*Theodore Roosevelt, address at the Capitol Building in Sacramento, California, May 19, 1903*

Panama gave the United States a six-mile (10 km) strip of land to build the Panama Canal. Eventually the canal would link the Atlantic and Pacific Oceans and vastly shorten the distance ships had to sail between the two oceans. Since its opening in 1914, the canal has been considered an engineering and construction marvel, as well as an economic necessity for worldwide trade.

Theodore's pace for getting things done as president was dizzying. Yet, he still had time for the "White House Gang," as many referred to Theodore's six children, who kept the president's home youthful and lively.[5] The entire family shared a love for animals. It was not unusual for dignitaries and diplomats visiting the White House to see Theodore's children chasing their pony through the halls. There was also a cat, Josiah the badger, Maude the pig, an assortment of dogs, a lizard, and a few other pets even Theodore forgot lived with the family. The press loved to write about these happenings as well as the activities of Theodore's oldest daughter, Alice, who made her social debut in the White House.

By his actions on both the domestic and foreign policy fronts, Theodore increased the power of the presidency. He won an overwhelming victory in the November 1904 election, garnering 56 percent of the popular vote against his Democratic opponent, Alton Parker. Theodore was happy he was no longer an "accidental president."[7]

The public loved hearing stories about the president's children.

The 1904 election gave Theodore a mandate of his own. He regulated national corporations that produced goods for public consumption, such as food, meat, and drugs. These companies' factories now had to meet sanitary requirements, and their products had to meet quality standards. Theodore protected the environment, creating five national parks and setting aside 230 million acres (93 million ha) of forest that could not be developed. Theodore also established the US Forest Service and numerous national monuments.[8]

THE BIG MOMENT

PEACEMAKER

Both Russia and Japan sought to expand their empires at the turn of the 1900s. This was of great concern to Theodore. He worried war between the two nations would alter the balance of power in the Pacific. As tensions between Russia and Japan reached a boiling point, Japan attacked the Russia Far East Naval Fleet in Port Arthur in southern Manchuria. War was declared between the two nations, and the Russo-Japanese War dragged on from February 1904 well into 1905.

During the summer of 1905, Theodore tried to get both sides to meet, with the goal of ending the conflict. Finally, in August, the warring nations sent representatives to a peace conference set up by Theodore in Portsmouth, New Hampshire. The president met with both sides at the start of the conference. Then he went to Oyster Bay and let the diplomats do their work. At a pivotal point in the four-week negotiations, Theodore invited

The president met with envoys from Russia and Japan in August 1905.

First the Japanese and then the Russians to Oyster Bay. There he met with both parties individually, secured compromises from representatives of each nation, and forged an agreement to end the war.

The Treaty of Portsmouth, signed on September 5, 1905, gave both nations a partial victory. It also boosted the power and prestige of the US presidency, showing the influence the commander in chief could have throughout the world. For his efforts, Theodore became the first American and the first US president to win the Nobel Peace Prize.

CHAPTER 6

PASSING THE
TORCH

November 1904 would be noteworthy for the Roosevelts for more than political reasons. Much to Theodore's delight, his niece Eleanor announced her engagement to Franklin Delano Roosevelt, her fifth cousin. The two had known each other as children and had spent time together at Theodore's home in Oyster Bay. They had rekindled their friendship in the summer of 1902, when they met by chance on a train traveling from New York City to Poughkeepsie, New York. After the train ride, the two agreed to correspond, and soon a romance blossomed.

Franklin was determined and confident, two traits Eleanor found appealing. His childhood had been very different from that of his future wife. Franklin was raised as an only child. There was a 28-year age

Franklin's formal portrait at age 18

difference between Franklin and his older half-brother, James. James was married and out of the house by the time Franklin was born.

Franklin's parents lavished a great deal of attention on him. It was the kind of childhood Eleanor dreamed of but never had. Unlike Eleanor, Franklin had to deal with very little sadness in his life while he was growing up. However, Franklin's father, James, died at age 72 during his son's first year in college.

Franklin modeled his life after that of his famous cousin, President Theodore Roosevelt, going as far as to attend and graduate from Harvard and go to Columbia Law School. Franklin planned to enter politics as well because, similar to Theodore, he found law boring.

A Power Couple

Franklin and Eleanor's engagement remained a secret at first. Franklin's mother, Sara, was not thrilled about her son's plans to marry Eleanor. She claimed that at 21 years old, her son was too young to wed. But in reality, Sara was very possessive of him. Franklin and Eleanor agreed to keep their marriage plans under wraps from Thanksgiving 1903, when they first told his mother of their desire to wed, until

Sara hoped Franklin and Eleanor would break up, but eventually she had to accept their engagement.

Thanksgiving 1904. The official announcement of Franklin and Eleanor's engagement came a few weeks after Theodore claimed victory in the 1904 presidential election.

Both Eleanor and Franklin had traits in common with Theodore. Well read, well mannered, and patient, Eleanor used her knowledge to volunteer and teach children on New York City's Lower East Side. Franklin had Theodore's political energy and moral convictions. Eleanor and Franklin seemed to be the perfect young power couple.

Franklin, who was a Democrat, voted for his Republican cousin Theodore and rejoiced in his victory. Franklin and Eleanor attended the inauguration of Theodore on March 4, 1905. A few weeks later, Theodore marched in the Saint Patrick's Day parade up Fifth Avenue in New York City on the morning of March 17. Later that day, he gave the bride away at Eleanor and Franklin's wedding.

The marriage of Franklin and Eleanor was not the only wedding in which Theodore played a major role. His eldest daughter, Alice, led a diplomatic delegation on a tour of Asia in July 1905. On the tour, Alice met Republican congressman Nicholas Longworth of Ohio. He was 16 years older than the 20-year-old First Daughter. However, on February 17, 1906, the couple married at the White House. It was the social event of the year, and it cemented Alice's place in Washington, DC, high society for the rest of her life.

When Theodore won the presidential election in 1904, he said afterward he would not seek another term. And he did not run in 1908. Instead, he threw his support behind his close friend and US secretary of war William Howard Taft. Theodore believed Taft was a fellow reformer and would uphold the Progressive ideals Theodore himself believed in. With Theodore's strong support, Taft easily won the presidency in November 1908, defeating his Democratic opponent William Jennings Bryan.

> **"We, here in America, hold in our hands the hope of the world, the fate of the coming years."[1]**
> —*Theodore Roosevelt, speaking at Carnegie Hall, New York City, March 20, 1912*

Meanwhile, Franklin and Eleanor were settling into family life. They had their first child, a daughter named Anna, in May 1906. Franklin was a father of two—Anna and a son, James II—by the time he took his first job as a lawyer with the prestigious Wall Street firm of Carter, Ledyard & Millburn. Franklin and Eleanor's third child, Franklin Jr., was born in March 1909. Both Franklin and Eleanor were devastated when Franklin Jr. died in infancy in November. The couple wanted to have another child as soon as possible. Elliott Roosevelt was born in September 1910.

That same year, Franklin had been asked to run for the New York State Senate from Dutchess County as a Democrat. Only one Democrat had won an election there since 1856. But Franklin was a Roosevelt. He had the aura of his famous name and the money to fund a strong campaign. Yet Franklin would not run as a Democrat unless he got Theodore's blessing.

Theodore believed he could count on Franklin to fight political bosses and corruption, no matter what party he was in. He told Franklin that while he would rather have him as a Republican, he did not mind if he ran as a Democrat. Franklin was overjoyed. His political career was about to begin.

A Natural Politician

Franklin was a vigorous and tireless campaigner. Much to everyone's surprise, he won election to the New York State Senate in 1910, at the age of 28. In 1911, shortly after being sworn in, Franklin took on political bosses to block a civil appointment. The standoff lasted for several months until a compromise candidate was chosen to replace the one favored by political bosses. Theodore was impressed by young Franklin's determination to curb bossism. What did not impress Theodore, or the American people, was the poor performance of the man in the White House, Theodore's successor, Taft.

Taft had aligned himself with the conservative wing of the Republican Party. Theodore felt Taft had betrayed the Progressives, not fighting for what he felt was best for the public welfare—for all workers, for women and children, consumers, the poor, the downtrodden, and immigrants. He charged that Taft failed to preserve the environment and cozied up to big business. He questioned Taft's resolve to fight corruption and political bosses.

Theodore Runs Again

In 1912, Theodore challenged Taft for the Republican presidential nomination, believing Taft did not deserve a second term. Theodore had substantial support but not enough to deprive Taft of the nomination. Undeterred, Theodore started a

LEARNING EXPERIENCE

When Franklin ran for the New York State Senate in 1910, he used the race as political training for the future. He tried innovative ways of campaigning. One was traveling through his election district in a car, which was unheard of at the time. He rented a red Maxwell automobile, put election banners all over it, and traveled to rural areas of his district. The car attracted a crowd and made meeting the candidate unforgettable. He introduced himself as Frank, a fellow resident. He went up to people with an outstretched hand, ready to greet them. He remembered small details, such as people's names and issues they had called to his attention. He spoke at large gatherings as much as possible during the campaign to strengthen his public speaking skills. Most important, he always had a smile on his face.

PROGRESSIVES

Industrial growth in the United States created an array of social, economic, and political problems by the turn of the 1900s. These problems desperately needed to be addressed, which is when the Progressive movement began picking up momentum.

Progressives were reformers who believed many of the problems facing the nation could be resolved through government regulation. The government was taking a hands-off approach to these issues. Progressives wanted the government to improve living conditions, expand public education, strengthen child labor laws, upgrade health and safety standards, end unfair labor practices, adopt consumer protection laws, give women the right to vote, conserve natural resources, and fight political corruption, among other things. Theodore believed in much of the Progressive agenda and was a lifelong supporter of the movement. When he was president, Theodore implemented many Progressive reforms.

third party, called the Progressive Party, and ran in the November 1912 presidential election against Taft, the incumbent Republican, and Woodrow Wilson, the Democrat, who was serving as governor of New Jersey. With the Republican Party split, Wilson won the White House.

The election split more than the Republican Party. Franklin publicly supported Wilson, angering the Oyster Bay branch of the family. Franklin's support of Wilson did not come as a surprise to Theodore. Theodore understood politics, and he knew Franklin was popular in the Democratic Party, especially in New York. Theodore was also well aware that Franklin had developed a strong friendship with Wilson, from

Theodore campaigns for the Progressive Party in 1912.

neighboring New Jersey. So Franklin's backing of Wilson was a logical career move.

Eleanor, meanwhile, would not criticize her uncle Theodore. Instead, she remained

loyal to him, insisting, "He had a feeling for social justice which was ahead of

his time."[2]

CHAPTER 7

POLITICAL SETBACKS

During the 1912 election, while Theodore battled to recapture the presidency, Franklin was seeking reelection to the New York State Senate. Unlike Theodore, Franklin claimed a victory. His second term in the New York State Senate, however, did not last long. President Wilson saw Franklin as a rising star in the Democratic Party. Wilson appointed the 31-year-old Franklin assistant secretary of the US Navy—the same federal post Theodore had held 12 years earlier. Franklin knew a great deal about the US Navy. This information would be vital in the upcoming years.

In late July 1914, war broke out in Europe. Anticipating the United States would be drawn into the war, Franklin worked to modernize the

Franklin had spent years studying the US Navy and researching the work Theodore had done while he was navy secretary.

US Navy, preparing it for international conflict. That meant increasing manpower and shifting from coal to oil to power the fleet. In March 1915, Franklin founded the US Navy Reserve. The concept of the reserves was for an expertly trained group of civilians to be ready to back up active navy personnel in the event of a war. The reserves still exist today.

DOWN BUT NOT OUT

When Franklin ran for reelection to the New York State Senate in 1912, he was seriously ill with typhoid fever. This bacterial infection caused weakness, fever, severe headaches, and abdominal pain. As a result, he could not campaign. Franklin hired newspaper reporter Louis Howe to handle his reelection bid and campaign for him. Franklin had done a great deal for his district and was popular and well liked. He easily won reelection without making a single campaign appearance. He completely recovered from the illness.

Franklin handled the pressures of his office with ease. He often argued with his boss, Navy Secretary Josephus Daniels, over readiness and strategy. Franklin refused to back down on issues involving the US Navy's ability to respond to hostilities around the world that posed a threat to the United States.

The First World War

That threat became a reality when the United States entered World War I (1914–1918) on April 6, 1917, in response to German aggression on the high seas. After German submarines sank four US merchant ships in March 1917, the United States joined the war on the side of the Allies, the United Kingdom, France, and Russia, who were fighting the Central powers, which included Germany, Austria-Hungary, the Ottoman Empire, and Bulgaria.

Franklin felt Wilson had waited too long to enter the war. Theodore agreed with his cousin. The former president had been pushing Wilson to take a forceful stance against Germany and the Central powers from the start of World War I. When the United States finally entered the war, Franklin felt his efforts to bolster the US Navy had positioned the nation to make a major contribution to winning the war.

Franklin wanted to fight in uniform as part of the armed forces during World War I. But Wilson asked him to

UNDER FIRE

The 1912 presidential campaign proved to be strenuous for all the candidates. But as a third-party candidate, Theodore gave more than 30 speeches each day, and nothing but a bullet could slow him down.[1]

On October 14, a deranged man named John Schrank shot Theodore outside the Gilpatrick Hotel in Milwaukee, Wisconsin. Theodore was hit in the chest, but the bullet missed all of his vital organs. His thick speech manuscript had slowed the bullet down. He insisted on delivering his hour-long speech with blood dripping down his shirt. After the speech, Theodore's aides had trouble getting him to go to a local hospital for emergency treatment. Edith finally made him stop campaigning to recover from the wound.

remain in his role as assistant US Navy secretary, a civilian position, because he was needed to make wartime decisions. Franklin was one of the most knowledgeable men in the country about the US Navy. Disappointed he would not be on the front lines, Franklin did everything he could to get as close to the battlefields of Europe as possible. He went on inspection tours in Europe, visiting US Navy ships and sailors as well as Allied military installations. Eleanor was busy as well, volunteering with the Red Cross.

The aging Theodore was intent on recruiting a volunteer regiment, similar to the Rough Riders, to fight in Europe. Theodore asked Wilson for permission to do that but was turned down. All four of Theodore's sons volunteered for military service and saw

BEHIND THE SCENES
UNFAITHFUL

In the summer of 1918, when World War I was still raging, Franklin went to Europe to inspect US naval vessels in the war zone. Upon his return in September, Eleanor was unpacking his bags and found a stack of love letters to Franklin from another woman. She was devastated. The woman was her one-time social secretary, Lucy Mercer.

Eleanor and Franklin decided not to seek a divorce. At the time, a divorce would have ruined his political career. Franklin promised to never see Mercer again. Despite this betrayal, Franklin and Eleanor became an effective political team, working together to combat social injustice and inequality.

action in Europe. Theodore's daughter Ethel also served in France as a nurse during the war.

The worst blow to the Roosevelt family came on July 14, 1918, when Theodore's youngest son, Quentin, an Army Air Corps pilot, was shot down in Germany and killed. When Theodore heard the news, he was stoic, but his closest friends said he never recovered from Quentin's death. The war ended in an Allied victory on November 11, 1918.

A New Era for the Roosevelts

By late 1918, Theodore had updated his Progressive agenda to include conservation of the nation's waterways and a bill of rights for returning military personnel. Theodore was planning another run for the White House in 1920. But his body failed him. On January 6, 1919, Theodore died in his sleep at age 60. His son Archie sent a cable to family members that read, "The old lion is dead."[2]

Franklin would take the national stage in 1920. The Democratic Party nominated Ohio Governor James M. Cox for president in 1920. Cox was not well known outside of Ohio. The party wanted a dynamic young candidate to balance the ticket and selected 37-year-old Franklin. Cox and Franklin lost to the Republican ticket of Warren G. Harding and Calvin Coolidge. The country was tired of war, and the Harding-Coolidge team promised a return to normalcy.

Franklin took his defeat on the presidential ticket in stride. However, the election loss meant he would not be in public office for the first time since 1910. He planned on returning to the political fray soon, but that decision would be out of his hands.

Although they lost the presidential race, Cox and Franklin, *right*, were an energetic duo during the campaign.

There was a Roosevelt victory in 1920, however. Theodore's eldest son, Ted, launched his political career by winning a seat as a Republican in the New York State Assembly. Harding then appointed Ted to be assistant secretary of the US Navy on March 10, 1921. Ted now held the same job his father, Theodore, and his cousin, Franklin, once held.

A Health Crisis

For years, Franklin and Eleanor's family vacationed on Campobello Island in New Brunswick, Canada. In August 1921, they were busy sailing, picnicking, and swimming. Their children loved the island, and Franklin now had time to be with them. On the afternoon of August 10, Franklin complained of chills and excruciating lower-back pain. He decided to go to bed early and sleep off what he thought was an oncoming cold.

When Franklin woke the next day, he had trouble moving his left leg. Then his right leg went limp. Three days later, most of Franklin's muscles from his chest down had become paralyzed. Local doctors could not diagnose what was wrong with the 39-year-old. After two weeks, the family sent for a specialist from Boston to examine Franklin. Dr. Robert W. Lovett concluded Franklin had polio, a harmful and often deadly disease.

In mid-September, Franklin, on a stretcher, made the long journey by boat and train from Canada to New York Presbyterian Hospital. He spent six weeks in the hospital, where the paralysis failed to improve. Franklin, however, was determined to recover from the disease and walk again.

Over the next several years, Franklin tried a variety of therapies in hopes of regaining the use of his legs. For all those years, he stayed out of the public eye.

After his polio diagnosis, Franklin needed the help of crutches, leg braces, or a wheelchair to move around.

Eleanor, together with Franklin's mother, Sara, worked hard to convince people Franklin was getting better. Franklin did the same. He felt it was essential if he was ever going to make a political comeback. Franklin's legs became frailer through the years. Even though doctors told him progress was unlikely, Franklin refused to accept his fate.

In 1926, Franklin purchased a resort in Warm Springs, Georgia, and turned it into a polio treatment center. It is still in operation today. He had his legs fitted with iron braces and taught himself, through a painful process,

FIGHTING BACK

There has not been a case of polio in the United States since 1979, but it was the most feared disease in the nation in the early and mid-1900s. Thousands of people were paralyzed or killed by this contagious viral illness. Polio mostly struck children, but it attacked adults as well, and Franklin was one of its adult victims.

To spare others from this devastating disease, Franklin founded the National Foundation for Infantile Paralysis in 1938. The foundation was created to fund research on polio and to help those afflicted by it. The organization became better known as the March of Dimes when the public was told that even contributing just a dime could help fight the disease. With funds from the March of Dimes, Dr. Jonas Salk developed a polio vaccine in 1953. Widespread use of the vaccine in the United States began in 1955.

to walk short distances in public. Privately, he used a wheelchair, but he was careful not to be seen using it in public. Franklin and his advisers felt the American public would never elect a candidate with a disability for any public office. The candidate would be viewed as sickly and weak, unable to fulfill the duties of the office.

Franklin stayed involved in politics, despite his health problems. Eleanor regularly gave speeches to civic groups and attended Democratic Party events, keeping Franklin's name in the public eye. She was active in the League of Women Voters and the Women's Trade Union League, both of which advocated for women's rights and helped shape public policy.

THE BIG MOMENT

THE ROAD BACK

The first few years Franklin battled polio were the toughest. In April 1924, the Democratic governor of New York, Al Smith, met with Franklin. Smith was seeking the Democratic nomination for president and asked Franklin to nominate him at the Democratic National Convention in late June. It would be Franklin's first major public appearance since 1921. Franklin accepted, but he insisted on walking to the podium to deliver the nomination speech.

For weeks, wearing his iron braces and using crutches in the privacy of his New York City home, Franklin practiced walking to the podium. His eldest son, James, walked with him.

At noon on June 26, 1924, Franklin was called to the podium. With the aid of crutches and holding James's arm, he walked slowly and deliberately to the microphones as 12,000 people looked on.[3] When he got to the podium, thunderous applause broke out.

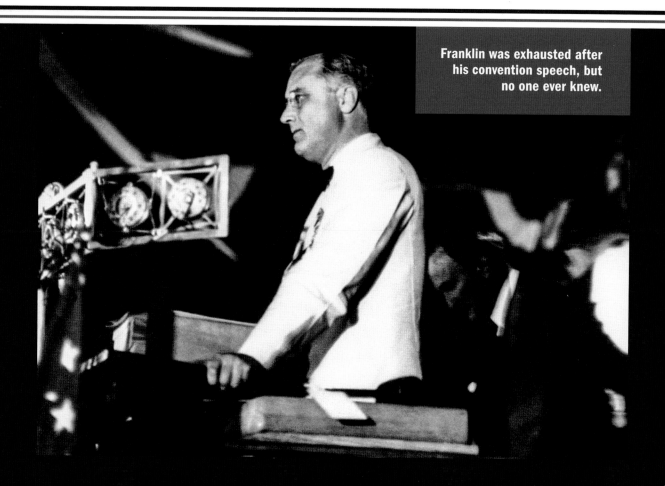

Franklin was exhausted after his convention speech, but no one ever knew.

Franklin's voice was strong. His words rang out through the hall and over radio stations carrying the speech live. Franklin stood for more than 30 minutes making the speech and then triumphantly walked off the stage, James at his side.

After a long political battle at the convention, Smith failed to gain the nomination. But all agreed that Franklin was the biggest winner at the convention.

> **"You gain strength, courage and confidence by every experience in which you really stop to look fear in the face. . . . You must do the thing you think you cannot do."[4]**
>
> —*Eleanor Roosevelt*

Eleanor was not comfortable with public speaking. She preferred working behind the scenes. But Franklin's illness pushed her into the spotlight. When speaking in public, she learned how to make eye contact and connect with her audience. She polished her delivery as she began giving more and more speeches. Her sincerity came through naturally; so did her passion. Soon, she saw audiences were responding to her. She began to enjoy her role at the podium. Eleanor spoke candidly and the audience related to her. While she always insisted she was working on Franklin's behalf, it did not take long for her to become acclaimed in her own right and to see her public appearances as a vehicle for social change. Meanwhile, with guidance from his close friend and adviser Louis Howe, Franklin began planning a return to politics.

Eleanor feared speaking in public at first and did not think she could do it.

CHAPTER 8

A LEADER IN DIFFICULT TIMES

By 1928, Franklin was back on the campaign trail, running for New York governor. For Franklin, who was still battling the effects of polio, the race was a gamble. A loss might end his political career. He drew big crowds wherever he went and addressed them standing up, usually from the backseat of his touring car. He did this by wearing braces under his trousers and holding a specially placed steel bar in the back of the car. Franklin appeared strong and vigorous, putting to rest any notion that he was too ill to serve.

Franklin won the New York governorship by a slim 25,000-vote margin on November 6, 1928.[1] It would be his first step on the road to the White House. As governor, Franklin wasted no time making reforms.

Franklin is sworn in as governor of New York with Eleanor behind him.

When he took office, the nation was on the verge of an economic crisis. New Yorkers were feeling the impact of the impending disaster, as was the rest of the nation. Franklin helped small farmers by putting tax cuts in place, boosting funding for rural education, expanding statewide social services, championing consumer rights by regulating businesses to eliminate unfair practices, and addressing New York's power problems by pushing to develop cheap hydroelectric power.

FAMILY FEUD

Before Franklin ran for governor of New York in 1928, Ted Jr., the eldest son of Theodore, ran for governor of New York in 1924 as a Republican. He took on the incumbent governor, Al Smith. Both Eleanor and Franklin came out against their cousin Ted. They cited his poor record as assistant secretary of the US Navy. Ted lost by 105,000 votes, and he never forgave his cousins for campaigning against him.[2] When Franklin ran for governor in 1928, he did not get the support of the Oyster Bay Roosevelts, but he won the office anyway.

Franklin became a master of the mass media, using radio and newspapers to keep the public informed about everything he was doing. He held press conferences twice a day. He also toured the state extensively. While Franklin met with farmers and local leaders, Eleanor visited hospitals and other state institutions. She reported what she saw to her husband, who took action based on her findings. For instance, at her husband's request Eleanor visited state prisons. She inspected the kitchens, checking that they were sanitary and the food being prepared was nourishing. She also made sure inmates in the facilities were being treated humanely.

Besides her duties as the First Lady of New York, Eleanor spent some of her time doing what she loved most: teaching. She and two friends had purchased the Todhunter School in 1926, and Eleanor taught history, literature, and public affairs

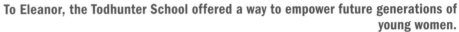
To Eleanor, the Todhunter School offered a way to empower future generations of young women.

to the students at the elite girls' school in New York City. The Todhunter School prepared young girls to carry on the fight for women's rights and social change.

The Great Depression

In the fall of 1929, the US economy started spiraling out of control. The New York Stock Exchange plunged drastically in October. A panic followed as investors tried to sell their stock holdings at any price. The stock market nearly collapsed, almost shutting down the nation's economy. Stocks became worthless, jobs were lost, people were afraid to spend money, and the pace of bank failures accelerated. This period became known as the Great Depression, the worst economic downturn in the nation's history.

Franklin and President Herbert Hoover differed on how to handle the crisis. Hoover felt the nation would rebound without intervention from the federal government. Franklin believed the government had to step in and lend its financial might to help people through this disaster by funding programs that provided jobs and relief to those struggling with the economic downturn.

At the time there were no government programs for the unemployed. Franklin persuaded the state legislature to pass the New York State Unemployment Relief Act.

He then set up the New York State Temporary Emergency Relief Administration to offer financial assistance to those in need.

Other states followed his lead as Franklin warned that government "owes the definite obligation to prevent the starvation or the dire want of any of its fellow men and women who try to maintain themselves but cannot."[3] As despair among the jobless grew and the economy worsened, Franklin decided to run against Hoover for the presidency in 1932.

Eleanor knew her husband could do the job, but she was uneasy about the prospect of constantly being the subject of national media attention. Nevertheless, she felt the nation needed Franklin in the White House. Pledging a New Deal for Americans, Franklin swept to victory on November 8. The New Deal involved a series of innovative federal programs intended to lay the foundation for economic stability and prosperity. Franklin

Franklin speaks to farmers in Topeka, Kansas, about the New Deal programs he promises to start as president.

THE FIRST 100 DAYS

Franklin's emergency measures in 1933, during his first 100 days in office, included establishment of the following:

- The National Recovery Administration (NRA), a partnership among government, industry, and labor to restore employment and overall prosperity. The NRA established competition between rival companies and fair wages and working conditions.

- The Public Works Administration, which created public works projects designed to employ millions.

- The Federal Emergency Relief Administration, which provided millions of dollars to states for work relief programs and direct public assistance.

- The Federal Deposit Insurance Corporation, which guaranteed bank deposits and strengthened the Federal Reserve Board's authority to regulate interest rates.

- The Agricultural Adjustment Administration, which helped farmers by boosting the price of farm products.

- The Federal Securities Act, the forerunner of the Securities Act of 1934. This established the Securities and Exchange Commission to regulate the stock market and stock sales.

- The Civilian Conservation Corps, which provided jobs for 250,000 young men in conservation and forestry.[4]

was committed to creating a structure to ensure economic growth, health, welfare, public well-being, and corporate responsibility.

Franklin took office on March 4, 1933, in the middle of a bank panic, when customers of many banks were withdrawing their money from those financial institutions. This destabilized the whole banking system. Franklin saw people were afraid to spend or invest money. He declared in his inaugural address, "The only thing we have to fear is fear itself—nameless, unreasoning, unjustified terror, which paralyzes needed efforts to convert retreat into advance."[5] Franklin was telling the nation that fear was leading the country to ruin. Instead of running from the problem, Americans could battle it and triumph over it by showing confidence in the banking system rather than giving up on it.

Five days later, Franklin presented Congress with the Emergency Banking Act as the first step to reassuring Americans the banking system was safe. It was passed immediately. This act increased Franklin's power to address banking

BANK RUNS

When depositors lose confidence in a bank, they withdraw their money. If a large majority of a bank's depositors withdraw their money at the same time, it is called a bank run. Banks only keep a fraction of the cash depositors have deposited there on hand. Most of the money is lent out to borrowers, who pay it back with interest. In the Depression, almost all bank customers wanted their money back at once. People felt their money would be safer at home than in a bank. Banks could not get the money back from their borrowers fast enough to cover all the withdrawals, and lost large sums of money trying to recover the money. As a result, many banks went out of business, often without paying back depositors. At the time, the federal government did not guarantee money in the banks, as it does today. The New Deal created such a system, and it remains in place.

emergencies and allowed the government to restrict the operations of a failed bank. Franklin explained how he stabilized the banking system in his first Fireside Chat, a radio broadcast to Americans, on March 12, 1933. By March 13, people started redepositing their money in neighborhood banks. The act ended the bank runs. But that only addressed one segment of the economic distress brought on by the Great Depression. Much more remained to be done.

With a 25 percent unemployment rate, the US economy was in a tailspin. Those who kept their jobs had to endure pay cuts, farm prices fell by 60 percent, and homelessness was rampant. During his first 100 days in office, Franklin got the US Congress to pass 15 major bills, which formed the basis of the New Deal: relief, recovery, and reform.[6] The bills were the result of the combined efforts of Franklin, his cabinet, and Congress.

Eleanor's Key Role

Franklin assembled a cabinet of top-notch experts in financial, economic, and social issues. One of the people whose counsel he sought most was Eleanor. She traveled around the country, visiting the people hit hardest by the Depression. The First Lady served as Franklin's eyes, ears, and legs. She gauged how well New Deal programs were working and told her husband where improvements were critically needed.

Knowledgeable and persistent, Eleanor addressed issues of inequality, poverty, and social injustice.

People felt comfortable talking to Eleanor. They told her their problems and what they needed. She received mail from people desperately seeking help. She passed those letters on to government officials and urged them to take action. She was never shy about telling her husband what she thought, using phrases such as "Franklin, I think you should . . ." or "Franklin, surely you will not . . ." He rarely said no to her, especially since she had the facts.[7]

MY DAY

Millions of Americans read a daily newspaper column Eleanor wrote. Called My Day, the column ran in daily newspapers throughout the country from late December 1935 to September 1962. My Day focused on pressing social and political issues, such as gender bias and racial injustice, and chronicled events during Franklin's presidency and beyond. The column dealt with everything from the effects of the Great Depression through World War II. In later years, the column even touched on topics such as the space program.

As the Great Depression wore on, the New Deal reforms did not go far enough to overcome stubborn unemployment and poverty. By 1935, the president introduced a new round of legislation to combat many of the persistent economic problems. Often referred to as the Second New Deal, this series of legislation included a jobs bill that provided funds to hire 2 million people and the Social Security Act, a measure designed to the help the elderly, the sick, and the poor.[8]

Franklin's 1936 reelection became a public vote on the First and Second New Deal reforms. Though newspapers and the Republican Party often criticized Franklin for spending government money to solve the nation's economic problems, Americans were solidly behind him. Franklin easily won a second term in 1936, defeating the Republican presidential candidate Alfred Landon. Franklin received 60.8 percent of the popular vote.[9]

Trouble Brewing Abroad

While Americans were focused on the economy and domestic issues, Franklin never lost sight of disturbing trends around the world. The Axis nations—Germany, Italy, and Japan—were determined to use military force to take over Europe, Asia, Africa, and islands in the Pacific Ocean. As early as 1937, Japan and Germany were preparing for a massive war. Franklin wanted to build up the US military in response. Isolationists in Congress were against that, insisting the nation remain neutral in the pending international conflict.

On March 12, 1938, Germany invaded and then occupied Austria, daring the world to respond. Nothing was done. For Franklin, the early signs of Japanese and German aggression signaled the magnitude of the conflict that lay ahead. He kept urging Congress to bolster the military.

Then, in the early morning hours of September 1, 1939, Franklin received a telephone call from William Bullitt, the US ambassador to France. Germany had invaded Poland. Franklin knew World War II (1939–1945) had started. "God help us all," Franklin told Bullitt.[11] Two days later, France and the United Kingdom, whose leaders had vowed to defend Poland if it were attacked, declared war on Germany.

Franklin warned Congress that aggression could not be fought by isolationism.

CHAPTER 9

TURBULENCE AND TRIUMPH

The United States did not feel the effects of World War II strongly until December 7, 1941, when Japan launched a surprise attack on the US naval base at Pearl Harbor, Hawaii. But the war weighed heavily on both Franklin and Eleanor long before that dark December day. Franklin promised he would do everything possible to keep the nation out of the war. However, he needed to stop the Axis powers from achieving global domination.

Modern civilization depended on the freedom of nations in Europe and the rest of the world, and the president believed the United States had an obligation to guard that freedom. "I do not belong to the school

The attack on Pearl Harbor spurred national support for entering the war.

of thought that says we can draw a line of defense around this country and live completely and solely to ourselves," he said.[1]

Despite Franklin's strongest efforts in 1939 and 1940, the US Congress was determined to keep the nation out of any conflict abroad, no matter how dire the

Franklin and Churchill spoke often over the course of World War II, discussing strategies and plans in case of a German attack.

situation overseas became. Still, Franklin found ways to help the Allies, especially the United Kingdom. He maintained an ongoing correspondence with Winston Churchill, the British First Lord of the Royal Navy. Together, they forged strategies for the United States to help the United Kingdom in the event the Nazis attacked the island nation. Churchill went on to become prime minister in May 1940.

Franklin continued urging Congress to increase the military budget because he knew the country would soon have to send weapons to the Allies. He also felt it was imperative for the United States to be able to respond immediately to any act of aggression against the nation. Congress reluctantly boosted military spending in 1939 as Franklin began converting the United States to a wartime economic footing. This would give the federal government the funds it needed to pay US manufacturers to make military equipment, such as ships and planes, for the war effort. Quietly, he had large manufacturers plan to convert their plants from peacetime production to wartime manufacturing. On November 4, 1939, Franklin also convinced Congress to allow the United States to sell arms to Allied European nations. There had been an embargo on those sales before.

Arms sales to the Allies had been banned because some members of Congress believed selling munitions to Allied nations would be viewed as an act of war by the Axis nations. These members of Congress concluded weapons sales would drag the United States into the war. In addition, there were members of the military who thought the United Kingdom would be defeated before the United States got into the war, and any weapons the United States sold to the British would fall into the hands of the Germans.

FOR WOMEN ONLY

As First Lady, Eleanor easily outdid her husband when it came to holding press conferences. Though First Ladies in the past had rarely spoken to the news media, Eleanor held 348 press conferences for women reporters only, the first one on March 6, 1933.[3] The press conferences were attended by the foremost female reporters of the time. Eleanor used the platform to publicize the work of women throughout the country and talk about major issues, such as race relations, youth activism, poverty, and war and peace. She entertained any questions the reporters had.

Eleanor's Humanitarian Efforts

In the late 1930s, Eleanor was working hard behind the scenes to lift immigration quotas to allow more refugees, especially Jews, to come to the United States. Reports of terrible persecution of Jews in Nazi-occupied nations had reached the White House. She lobbied hard for the passage of the Child Refugee Bill, which would have allowed 10,000 Jewish children per year to enter the United States over a two-year period.[2] Congress refused to pass the bill.

After the Night of Broken Glass, in which Nazi troops burned down synagogues and destroyed Jewish-owned businesses throughout German-occupied territory on November 9–10, 1938, Eleanor began working feverishly with numerous refugee rescue organizations. These included the Emergency Rescue Committee, the US Committee for the Care of European Children, and the Children's Crusade for Children. She managed to help refugees on an individual basis but was unable to change laws that would have permitted increased immigration overall.

Eleanor often received criticism for her work, even within her husband's administration. Breckinridge Long, assistant secretary of state for the Special War Problems Division, the person in charge of issuing visas, admitted his policy was to postpone as long as possible when it came to expanding quotas for immigration.

A Third Term?

Meanwhile, there was question as to who would be president in 1940. No US president had served more than two terms up to that point. Franklin was looking forward to retiring and taking on the role of elder statesman. However, the world was engulfed in an international crisis, and Franklin believed only he had the experience to guide the country through it.

In April 1940, Germany invaded Denmark and Norway. In early May, the Germans tore through the Netherlands, Belgium, and Luxembourg. By May 14, they had smashed through France, crushing French resistance. Americans were shocked by the rapid defeat of the French at the hands of the Nazis. Then Germany began air raids on England.

> **"It is common sense to take a method and try it. If it fails, admit it frankly and try another. But above all, try something."[5]**
> —*Franklin Roosevelt, in a speech at Oglethorpe University, May 22, 1932*

Even staunch isolationists realized US forces would eventually be drawn into World War II. Though some were against Franklin running for a third term, there was also a wave of support within his own party for him to stay on the job in these frightening times. Franklin sent a message to delegates at the 1940 Democratic National Convention in Chicago in mid-July. He said he would not run unless he was drafted and told the delegates they were free to vote for anyone. That message was read on the convention floor. It was followed by chants of "We want Roosevelt!" Franklin received the nomination on the first vote.[4]

By the summer of 1940, the United Kingdom was desperate for assistance. In September, Franklin sent 50 destroyers to aid the United Kingdom. He took action even though it made him appear to be pro-war right before Election Day. He was running against an antiwar Republican Wendell Willkie. His wartime support for the United Kingdom did not hurt Franklin at the polls, though, and he won the election on November 5 by 55 percent of the popular vote.[6]

Wartime President

Franklin gave a call to arms in a radio address on December 29, 1940. He said the United States was an "arsenal of democracy," and he promised to help the United Kingdom defeat Germany.[7] By the time he made this speech, Japan had signed a pact with Italy and Germany, vowing to defend one another if any one of the three Axis nations were attacked.

> **"We must remember that any oppression, any injustice, any hatred, is a wedge designed to attack our civilization."[8]**
> —*Franklin Roosevelt, in a letter to Dr. William Allan Neilson, January 9, 1940*

The United States stayed out of World War II for another year. But when Japan's ships and warplanes made their way to Pearl Harbor, Hawaii, in the early morning hours of December 7, 1941, to launch a surprise attack on the United States, the uneasy peace was shattered.

On December 8, Franklin addressed a joint session of Congress in what became known as the "Day of Infamy" speech. He declared, "Yesterday, December 7, 1941—a date which will live in infamy—the United States of America was suddenly and deliberately attacked by naval and air forces of the Empire of Japan."[9] He went on to say the United States had been at peace with Japan at the time of the attack. He told Congress that as the commander in chief of the US Army and Navy, he directed that all measures be taken for the nation's defense. Within one hour after Franklin was done speaking, Congress declared war on Japan. In keeping with their pact, Germany and Italy then declared war on the United States on December 11. The United States was now fully engaged in World War II.

Though angered by the attack on Pearl Harbor, Americans were also shaken by it. When the United States first joined the Allies in World War II, they were facing a tough task. Axis troops had taken over a great deal of territory in Europe, Asia, and North Africa and had the upper hand as US troops made their way to the battlefield.

Franklin inspired the nation at this difficult time. He gave both civilians and the military confidence that by following a determined, steady path, the Allies would win the war. In June 1942, after a string of defeats at the hands of the Japanese, the US Pacific Fleet won the battle of Midway, an important victory in the war in the Pacific. By 1943, the tide began to turn, and the Allies started beating enemy troops on all fronts.

Though Franklin was in declining health, he ran for a fourth term in 1944 and won. He had hoped to live to see an end to the war. He died on April 12, 1945, at the age

ANIMAL COMPANION

The World War II years were extremely stressful for Franklin. His dog, Fala, became a source of joy and comic relief for the president. A male Scottish terrier, the dog was a gift from Franklin's cousin, Margaret "Daisy" Suckley. Fala went everywhere with Franklin and became one of the most famous presidential pets ever. His antics were widely covered by the media, and he learned to be ready to leave the White House on a moment's notice. He traveled easily on planes, in boats, and in cars.

Fala outlived the president by seven years and was heartbroken when Franklin died. He became close to Eleanor, who often wrote about him in her column, My Day. Fala was buried next to Franklin in Hyde Park, New York, and has a statue in his honor as part of the Franklin Delano Roosevelt Memorial in Washington, DC.

of 63, in Warm Springs, where he had gone to rest in hopes of regaining his strength. Eleanor broke the news of the president's death to Vice President Harry S. Truman. Truman led the nation through the end of the war later that year. Victory in Europe was declared a short time after Franklin's death on May 8. Japan surrendered on August 15 after the United States dropped two atomic bombs on Japan.

Eleanor continued to have an extremely active life following Franklin's death. After taking time to mourn, she resumed a busy public speaking schedule. In December 1945, President Truman appointed her a delegate to the newly formed United Nations (UN) General Assembly. This appointment was an indication of how vital Truman felt the UN was to world peace. The UN had only been created two months before Eleanor was appointed, and the former First Lady gave credibility to the world body. In 1946, she became the chairperson of the UN Commission on Human Rights and spearheaded the passage of the Universal Declaration of Human Rights by the UN General Assembly in December 1948. The Universal Declaration was critical because it was one of the first documents the UN issued. It spelled out the rights the organization felt should be guaranteed to human beings throughout the world, among them life, liberty, and freedom of thought and expression. These were principles the United Nations wanted member nations to uphold. They were also the guiding principles of Eleanor's life.

Eleanor left her post at the UN in 1953. After, she continued to speak out about human rights and women's rights and visited nations throughout the world to promote peace. She also gave lectures, wrote books

Eleanor enjoyed her work with the UN and felt it was making a difference in people's lives.

and articles, supported the cause of civil rights, and worked tirelessly to lift people out of poverty.

President John F. Kennedy often consulted Eleanor about civil rights and the rights of women. Dignitaries from throughout the world sought her insight and views on a range of issues. She chaired the Presidential Commission on the Status of Women from December 1961 until her death on November 7, 1962, at the age of 78.

The Roosevelt Legacy

Theodore, mainly through the force of his personality, changed the presidency into a strong, effective executive position. He made the presidency the center of the political universe in the United States. From the bully pulpit, the chief executive could now be a reformer. He took on the titans of industry; fought for the rights of workers, tenants, children, and women; revolutionized the role of the United States in world affairs; and was the first driving force for environmental conservation.

Franklin's greatest achievement was keeping the United States from financial ruin during the Great Depression and securing the nation's economic infrastructure for the future. He also built the United States into a military and economic superpower. He was a symbol of enormous strength.

Eleanor championed the rights of the downtrodden, gave a voice to the voiceless, and proved women have a vital contribution to make in the political arena and society in general. She transformed the role of the First Lady from a ceremonial position to a job that affected people's lives on a daily basis. She was a role model for millions of girls and women throughout the world. Though she faced numerous challenges and did not always succeed in her efforts, Eleanor taught the world never to give up.

Two of Franklin and Eleanor's sons served in the US House of Representatives. James was elected to Congress from California in 1954 and reelected five times. Franklin Jr. represented New York in Congress from 1949 through 1955.

Since that time, the Roosevelt family has not been in the political spotlight. In 1986, James Roosevelt Jr., a grandson of Franklin, ran for the congressional seat being vacated by then–Speaker of the House Thomas P. O'Neill. He lost in the Democratic primary to Joseph P. Kennedy III, nephew of the late president John F. Kennedy. But James remains a member of the Democratic National Committee and is cochair of its Rules and Bylaws Committee. Despite their recent political fortunes, members of the Roosevelt family are still involved in humanitarian efforts, such as the Roosevelt Warm Springs Institute for Rehabilitation, and they are treated like royalty throughout the United States.

Franklin and Eleanor surrounded by their family in 1932

1858

Theodore Roosevelt is born on October 27.

1880

Theodore marries Alice Lee on October 27.

1882

Franklin Delano Roosevelt is born on January 30.

1889

Theodore is named civil service commissioner.

1898

Colonel Theodore leads the Rough Riders up San Juan Hill in Cuba on July 1.

1900

Theodore is elected US vice president on November 6.

1901

President William McKinley is shot on September 6 and dies on September 13; Theodore becomes US president.

1904

Theodore is elected president in November.

1905

Franklin and Eleanor Roosevelt are married on March 17.

1910

Franklin is elected to the New York State Senate in November.

1919

Theodore dies on January 6.

1924

Franklin nominates Al Smith for president at the Democratic National Convention on June 26, his first public appearance since contracting polio.

1928

Franklin makes a political comeback by being elected governor of New York on November 6.

1932

Franklin is elected president of the United States on November 8 in the midst of the Great Depression.

1933

Franklin takes office on March 4 and launches the New Deal to combat the effects of the Great Depression.

1935

Eleanor begins writing her My Day column at the end of December.

1940

Franklin is elected to an unprecedented third term as president on November 5.

1944

Franklin wins a fourth term as president in November.

1945

Franklin dies on April 12; President Harry S. Truman appoints Eleanor as a delegate to the United Nations General Assembly in December.

1948

Eleanor spearheads the passage of the Universal Declaration of Human Rights by the UN General Assembly in December.

1962

Eleanor dies on November 7.

- Theodore wore glasses because he was nearsighted. When he served with the Rough Riders, he had 12 pairs of glasses sewn into his uniform to make sure he would never lose sight of the enemy.[1]

- Theodore was the first US president to ride in an automobile in public on August 22, 1902. Up until that time, presidents made public appearances riding in a horse and carriage. He was also the first president to own a car.

- Theodore authored more than 35 books throughout his life.[2]

- Theodore wrote hundreds of letters, many to his children. He filled those letters with advice he hoped would serve his children throughout their lifetime. Theodore's children saved the letters, and quotes from them appear in various books.

- To honor Franklin for his service to the nation and his work with the March of Dimes, his image was put on the dime in 1946.

Franklin was an avid stamp collector. His collection included more than 1.2 million stamps.[3] Franklin's mother, Sara, also collected stamps. When Sara died, her collection was passed down to Franklin.

When Eleanor attended Allenswood, the all-girls' school in England, she played varsity field hockey.

Eleanor had an interest in flying and was a good friend of aviation pioneer Amelia Earhart.

Eleanor wrote 27 books and more than 580 articles. In addition, she was a guest on more than 300 radio and television shows.[4]

civil service
The government workforce at all levels.

corruption
Dishonesty and fraud in government.

destroyer
A versatile, fast, heavily armed warship.

elder statesman
A retired government leader who advises those currently in office.

embargo
A ban on selling particular products.

front
In war, a region where a battle is being fought.

Great Depression
The worst economic downturn in US history (1929–1941).

incumbent
An official currently in office.

mandate
The authority to carry out a policy or action.

New Deal
Franklin Roosevelt's plan of relief, recovery, and reform to get the United States out of the Great Depression.

patronage
The practice of giving out political jobs to unqualified people who do favors for those in public office.

political boss
Someone who runs a political party.

posthumous
After death.

reform
To make changes.

regiment
A military unit, usually commanded by a colonel.

restraint of trade
The practice by one corporation of preventing other corporations in the same field from conducting business.

stock
A share of the value of a company, which can be bought, sold, or traded.

trust
A combination of corporations, also known as a monopoly, that threatens to reduce competition and controls a large segment of the economy.

SELECTED BIBLIOGRAPHY

Beasley, Maurine H. *Eleanor Roosevelt: Transformative First Lady.* Lawrence, KS: UP of Kansas, 2010. Print.

Donald, Aida D. *Lion in the White House: A Life of Theodore Roosevelt.* New York: Basic, 2007. Print.

Goodwin, Doris Kearns. *The Bully Pulpit: Theodore Roosevelt, William Howard Taft, and the Golden Age of Journalism.* New York: Simon, 2013. Print.

FURTHER READINGS

Collard, Sneed B. *Eleanor Roosevelt: Making the World a Better Place.* New York: Marshall Cavendish, 2009.

Marrin, Albert. *FDR and the American Crisis.* New York: Knopf, 2015.

Sharp, Arthur G., *The Everything Theodore Roosevelt Book: The Extraordinary Life of an American Icon.* Avon, MA: Adams, 2011. Print.

WEBSITES

To learn more about America's Great Political Families, visit **booklinks.abdopublishing.com**. These links are routinely monitored and updated to provide the most current information available.

PLACES TO VISIT

HOME OF FRANKLIN D. ROOSEVELT

4097 Albany Post Road

Hyde Park, New York 12538

845-229-9115

http://www.nps.gov/hofr/index.htm

This is the home of Franklin and Eleanor Roosevelt. Visitors to this national historic site can tour the home, the presidential library and museum, the gardens, and several other historic buildings used by the family.

THEODORE ROOSEVELT INAUGURAL SITE

641 Delaware Avenue

Buffalo, New York 14202

716-884-0095

http://www.trsite.org

The home where Theodore Roosevelt was inaugurated following the assassination of President William McKinley is now a museum. Among the displays are items from the Pan-American Exposition where McKinley was shot on September 6, 1901.

CHAPTER 1. ROUGH RIDERS

1. Richard Flint and Shirley Cushing Flint. "Roosevelt's Rough Riders–1898." *New Mexico History.org.* Office of the State Historian, n.d. Web. 14 Aug. 2015.

2. "Chronology of Cuba in the Spanish-American War." *World of 1898.* Library of Congress, 22 June 2011. Web. 14 Aug. 2015.

3. Edward J. Renehan Jr. "The Lion's Pride." *New York Times.* New York Times Company, 1998. Web. 14 Aug. 2015.

CHAPTER 2. THEODORE'S WORLD

1. "Program Transcript." *American Experience.* WGBH Educational Network, 2013. Web. 14 Aug. 2015.

CHAPTER 3. A NEW FAMILY BUSINESS

1. Arthur G. Sharp. *The Everything Theodore Roosevelt Book: The Extraordinary Life of an American Icon.* Avon, MA: Adams Media, 2011. Print. 30.

2. Theodore Roosevelt. *Theodore Roosevelt, An Autobiography.* New York: Charles Scribner's Sons, 1920. Print. 44.

3. Aida D. Donald. *Lion in the White House: A Life of Theodore Roosevelt.* New York: Basic, 2007. Print. 41.

4. "Anna Roosevelt." *National Park Service.* National Park Service, 14 Aug. 2015. Web. 14 Aug. 2015.

5. Doris Kearns Goodwin. *The Bully Pulpit: Theodore Roosevelt, William Howard Taft, and the Golden Age of Journalism.* New York: Simon, 2013. Print. 137.

CHAPTER 4. A HERO COMES ALONG

1. "Our Mission, Role & History." *OPM.gov.* US Office of Personnel Management, n.d. Web. 14 Aug. 2015.

2. Aida D. Donald. *Lion in the White House: A Life of Theodore Roosevelt.* New York: Basic, 2007. Print. 62–63.

3. Ibid. 105.

4. Edward Stratemeyer. "American Boy's Life of Theodore Roosevelt." *Project Gutenberg.* Project Gutenberg, n.d. Web. 14 Aug. 2015.

5. James MacGregor Burns and Susan Dunn. *The Three Roosevelts: Patrician Leaders Who Transformed America.* New York: Atlantic Monthly, 2001. Print. 59.

6. "Roosevelt Completes One of Most Remarkable Campaigns Ever Made." *California Digital Newspaper Collection.* Digital Library Consulting, 2013. Web. 14 Aug. 2015.

7. Donald J. Davidson, ed. *The Wisdom of Theodore Roosevelt.* New York: Citadel, 2003. Print. 10.

8. Aida D. Donald. *Lion in the White House: A Life of Theodore Roosevelt.* New York: Basic, 2007. Print. 132.

CHAPTER 5. THE PEOPLE'S PRESIDENT

1. James MacGregor Burns and Susan Dunn. *The Three Roosevelts: Patrician Leaders Who Transformed America.* New York: Atlantic Monthly, 2001. Print. 71.

2. Ibid. 75.

3. H. W. Brands. *T. R.: The Last Romantic.* New York: Basic, 1997. Print. 509.

4. "Keynote of President Roosevelt's Labor Platform." *Current Literature.* Current Literature, 1904. Web. 14 Aug. 2015.

5. Aida D. Donald. *Lion in the White House: A Life of Theodore Roosevelt.* New York: Basic, 2007. Print. 182–184.

6. "Address at the Capitol Building in Sacramento, California." *American Presidency Project.* Gerhard Peters and John T. Woolley, 2015. Web. 14 Aug. 2015.

7. "Presidential Elections." *History.* A&E Television Networks, 2015. Web. 14 Aug. 2015.

8. "Program Transcript." *American Experience.* WGBH Educational Network, 2013. Web. 14 Aug. 2015.

CHAPTER 6. PASSING THE TORCH

1. *Senate Documents*. Washington, 1912. *Google Book Search*. Web. 14 Aug. 2015.

2. James MacGregor Burns, and Susan Dunn. *The Three Roosevelts: Patrician Leaders Who Transformed America*. New York: Atlantic Monthly, 2001. Print. 129.

CHAPTER 7. POLITICAL SETBACKS

1. Geoffrey C. Ward. *The Roosevelts: An Intimate History*. New York: Alfred A. Knopf, 2014. Print. 180–181.

2. Aida D. Donald. *Lion in the White House: A Life of Theodore Roosevelt*. New York: Basic, 2007. Print. 265.

3. Geoffrey C. Ward, ed. *Closest Companion: The Unknown Story of the Intimate Friendship between Franklin Roosevelt and Margaret Suckley*. Boston: Houghton, 1995. Print. 252.

4. Eleanor Roosevelt. *You Learn By Living*. New York: Harper, 1960. Print. 29–30.

CHAPTER 8. A LEADER IN DIFFICULT TIMES

1. James MacGregor Burns, and Susan Dunn. *The Three Roosevelts: Patrician Leaders Who Transformed America*. New York: Atlantic Monthly, 2001. Print. 193–195.

2. Ibid. 190.

3. Ibid. 213.

4. Alonzo L. Hamby. *For the Survival of Democracy: Franklin Roosevelt and the World Crisis of the 1930s*. New York: Free, 2004. Print. 126–129.

5. James MacGregor Burns and Susan Dunn. *The Three Roosevelts: Patrician Leaders Who Transformed America*. New York: Atlantic Monthly, 2001. Print. 251–254.

6. Paul S. Boyer, et al. *The Enduring Vision: A History of the American People*. Boston: Cengage Learning, 2011. Print. 743.

7. "Questions and Answers about Eleanor Roosevelt." *Eleanor Roosevelt Papers Project*. George Washington University, n.d. Web. 14 Aug. 2015.

8. James MacGregor Burns and Susan Dunn. *The Three Roosevelts: Patrician Leaders Who Transformed America*. New York: Atlantic Monthly, 2001. Print. 296–297.

9. Ibid. 307–315.

10. "Address at Madison Square Garden, New York City." *American Presidency Project*. Gerhard Peters and John T. Woolley, 2015. Web. 14 Aug. 2015.

11. James MacGregor Burns and Susan Dunn. *The Three Roosevelts: Patrician Leaders Who Transformed America*. New York: Atlantic Monthly, 2001. Print. 418–419.

CHAPTER 9. TURBULENCE AND TRIUMPH

1. James MacGregor Burns and Susan Dunn. *The Three Roosevelts: Patrician Leaders Who Transformed America.* New York: Atlantic Monthly, 2001. Print. 416.

2. "Anna Eleanor Roosevelt." *Eleanor Roosevelt Papers Project.* George Washington University, n.d. Web. 14 Aug. 2015.

3. Maurine H. Beasley. *Eleanor Roosevelt: Transformative First Lady.* Lawrence, KS: UP of Kansas, 2010. Print. 81.

4. *LIFE.* New York, 29 July 1940. *Google Book Search.* Web. 14 Aug. 2015.

5. "Address at Oglethorpe University, May 22, 1932." *Works of Franklin D. Roosevelt.* New Deal Network, 2015. Web. 14 Aug. 2015.

6. James MacGregor Burns and Susan Dunn. *The Three Roosevelts: Patrician Leaders Who Transformed America.* New York: Atlantic Monthly, 2001. Print. 428.

7. Geoffrey C. Ward. *The Roosevelts: An Intimate History.* New York: Knopf, 2014. Print. 378.

8. The Library of Congress. *Respectfully Quoted: A Dictionary of Quotations.* Mineola, NY, 2010. *Google Book Search.* Web. 14 Aug. 2015.

9. "Franklin D. Roosevelt's Infamy Speech." *University of Oklahoma College of Law.* University of Oklahoma College of Law, 2009. Web. 14 Aug. 2015.

FUN FACTS

1. Nancy Whitelaw. *Theodore Roosevelt Takes Charge.* Morton Grove, IL, 1992. *Google Book Search.* Web. 14 Aug. 2015.

2. Aida D. Donald. *Lion in the White House: A Life of Theodore Roosevelt.* New York: Basic, 2007. Print. 29.

3. "How They Collected: Franklin Delano Roosevelt." *Stamps.* USPS, 17 Apr. 2014. Web. 14 Aug. 2015.

4. "About the Project: Overview." *Eleanor Roosevelt Papers Project.* George Washington University, n.d. Web. 14 Aug. 2015.

Robert Grayson is an award-winning former daily newspaper reporter and the author of books for young adults. Throughout his journalism career, Grayson has written stories on historical figures, big-time athletes, arts and entertainment, businesses, politics, and pets, which have appeared in national and regional publications including the *New York Yankees* magazine and *NBA Hoop.* He has written biographies of environmental activists and professional sports figures as well as books about animals in the military, animal performers, law enforcement, and historic events.